How To Use This Study Guide

This five-lesson study guide corresponds to *"Taste and See That the Lord Is Good" With Rick Renner* (**Renner TV**). Each lesson in this study guide covers a topic that is addressed during the program series, with questions and references supplied to draw you deeper into your own private study of the Scriptures on this subject.

To derive the most benefit from this study guide, consider the following:

First, watch or listen to the program prior to working through the corresponding lesson in this guide. (Programs can also be viewed at **renner.org** by clicking on the Media/Archives links or on our Renner Ministries YouTube channel.)

Second, take the time to look up the scriptures included in each lesson. Prayerfully consider their application to your own life.

Third, use a journal or notebook to make note of your answers to each lesson's Study Questions and Practical Application challenges.

Fourth, invest specific time in prayer and in the Word of God to consult with the Holy Spirit. Write down the scriptures or insights He reveals to you.

Finally, take action! Whatever the Lord tells you to do according to His Word, do it.

For added insights on this subject, it is recommended that you obtain the book ***Our Healing Covenant*** by Dr. Chip Beaulieu. You may also select from Rick's other available resources by placing your order at **renner.org** or by calling 1-800-742-5593.

LESSON 1

TOPIC
We Are Partakers of Divine Sonship

SCRIPTURES
1. **Psalm 34:8** — O taste and see that the Lord is good: blessed is the man that trusteth in him.
2. **John 1:12** — But as many as received him, to them gave he power to become the sons of God, even to them that believe on his name.
3. **John 1:13** — Which were born, not of blood, nor of the will of the flesh, nor of the will of man, but of God.

GREEK WORDS
1. "but" — δέ (*de*): an exclamatory statement; to sound the alarm
2. "as many" — ὅσος (*hosos*): as great as or as much as; an unlimited number
3. "received" — λαμβάνω (*lambano*): to seize or lay hold of something in order to make it your own; to grab, capture, or take possession; one who graciously receives something that is freely and easily given
4. "gave" — δίδωμι (*didomi*): to supply; to bestow as a gift to one who is asking; to commit, to entrust, or to give into one's care
5. "power" — ἐξουσία (*exousia*): influence; delegated authority
6. "to become" — γίνομαι (*ginomai*): an initiated change that leads to a transition of one thing to another
7. "sons" — τέκνον (*teknon*): non-adult children who are still under parental guidance at home; children under the authority of a guardian
8. "on" — εἰς (*eis*): into; carries the idea of a merger
9. "name" — ὄνομα (*onoma*): denotes a person's character or reputation that distinguishes him from others

SYNOPSIS
The five lessons in this study guide titled *Taste and See That the Lord Is Good* will focus on the following topics:

A Note From Rick Renner

I am on a personal quest to see a "revival of the Bible" so people can establish their lives on a firm foundation that will stand strong and endure the test as end-time storm winds begin to intensify.

In order to experience a revival of the Bible in your personal life, it is important to take time each day to read, receive, and apply its truths to your life. James tells us that if we will continue in the perfect law of liberty — refusing to be forgetful hearers, but determined to be doers — we will be blessed in our ways. As you watch or listen to the programs in this series and work through this corresponding study guide, I trust you will search the Scriptures and allow the Holy Spirit to help you hear something new from God's Word that applies specifically to your life. I encourage you to be a doer of the Word He reveals to you. Whatever the cost, I assure you — it will be worth it.

> Thy words were found, and I did eat them;
> and thy word was unto me the joy and rejoicing of mine heart:
> for I am called by thy name, O Lord God of hosts.
> — Jeremiah 15:16

Your brother and friend in Jesus Christ,

Rick Renner

Unless otherwise indicated, all scripture quotations are taken from the *King James Version* of the Bible.

Taste and See That the Lord Is Good

Copyright © 2023 by Rick Renner
1814 W. Tacoma St.
Broken Arrow, OK 74012-1406

Published by Rick Renner Ministries
www.renner.org

ISBN 13: 978-1-6675-0308-0

eBook ISBN 13: 978-1-6675-0309-7

All rights reserved. No portion of this book may be reproduced or transmitted in any form or by any means — electronic, mechanical, photocopy, recording, scanning, or other — except for brief quotations in critical reviews or articles, without the prior written permission of the Publisher.

- We Are Partakers of Divine Sonship
- We Are Partakers of the Divine Nature
- We Are Partakers of Divine Deliverance
- We Are Partakers of Divine Healing
- We Are Partakers of Divine Provision

To understand Psalm 34:8 and truly "taste and see" for oneself that the Lord is good, he or she must *partake* of the blessings that He easily, freely, and graciously gives — *sonship, His divine nature, deliverance, healing*, and *financial provision*. Partaking of *divine sonship* means you've called upon Jesus as Lord and you're beginning to walk out the fullness of what that really means. Do you know what happened to you at the moment of your salvation? You were delivered from Satan's authority and you came under Christ's authority and rule. You traded darkness for light, and you now have *influence* in the realm of the spirit that was given to you by God. This lesson details how to become born again — how to lay hold of the power to enter into union with the character of Jesus Himself. A holy "merger" takes place in that act and you become one with Him.

The emphasis of this lesson:

It's not enough just to believe that Jesus is Lord. To partake of divine sonship, you must also make a profession of faith and actually call Him your Lord. And it's not enough just to be born again if you want to really "taste" of this blessing of sonship. You need to know what happened in that divine moment when you were removed from the authority of darkness and brought into the light of Christ's love.

Psalm 34:8 says, "O taste and see that the Lord is good…." The Lord is good, and He wants us to "taste" of Him and to partake of Him and all His blessings. In this lesson, we're going to be looking at *partaking of the blessing of divine sonship*.

In this program, Rick gave the testimony of his own salvation that occurred at a very young age.

> I was saved when I was five years old. I actually came into the realization of my need to be saved when I was four. My parents raised me in church. My mother taught me the Bible, and every night when I was young, my mother would lie down by my side,

and she would talk to me about salvation. She would talk to me about Heaven, and she would talk to me about hell. I'm so thankful that my mother did that because she prepared my heart from a very young age to be ready to receive Jesus.

We had an evangelist come preach in our church during a week of revival meetings. He preached every night, and one night he preached on the subject of hell. And what he preached about hell was so impacting that I could envision hell in my imagination.

He vividly described the fires of hell engulfing people, and I could *see* that in my mind's eye. As he preached, I came under great conviction of sin, and I wanted to go forward and give my heart to Christ, but I was just four years old. My mother, though she'd been talking to me about my salvation, was a little concerned that maybe I was too young — that it was too quick, too early, and I really didn't understand what I was doing. So she held me back.

About a year had passed and for that entire year, every night when I went to bed, I was fearful that if I died in my sleep, I would go to hell. And I would have because I had already come to the age of accountability. I understood sin, and I understood God's command to repent and to turn to Him.

Finally, one day in church, as I was sitting with my sister about halfway back in the auditorium, our pastor began to preach on salvation. Soon, the altar call came and the congregation began to sing. And I felt the Holy Spirit tugging on my heart.

I remember gripping the pew in front of me thinking about what it would feel like to walk the aisle in front of all those people. *Should I? Should I not?* My mother and daddy were in the choir; I could see them right in front of me. But, finally, the moment came when I released that pew. I slipped out from my place into the aisle and walked down to the front.

My pastor's name was Brother Post, and he said, "Ricky, why are you here?" I said, "Brother Post, I'm here to give my heart to Jesus." I went over to the front pew and waited for my Sunday School teacher, named Jerry. What an impact that Sunday School teacher had on my life!

(By the way, never underestimate your role in the local church. You're impacting people *you don't even know about!*) Jerry and I got on our knees, and he led me in a prayer of repentance. Before I knew it, my parents had slipped out of the choir and came down to the front to be with me as I made my public profession of faith.

Back in those days, we wasted no time when it came to water baptism. Brother Post came to our house that very afternoon to talk to me and make sure I understood what I had done that morning so I could be water baptized later that night. And when the time for the evening service came, I went to the baptistry to be baptized.

Because I was so young and little in size, people in the auditorium couldn't see my head in the baptistry, so Brother Post brought me a metal chair to stand on so the crowd could see my head just barely poking above the rail of the baptistery. He then baptized me in the name of the Father, the Son, and the Holy Ghost. And that started my new life in Christ that day.

But when I got saved, I did not understand what a miracle had taken place in my life. *Most people* who get saved don't understand what really transpired, but it is the greatest miracle that can ever take place. But on that day, I was born of God.

Now, let me ask you — on the day you got saved, did you truly understand what happened inside you? Of course you didn't — you were literally rescued from darkness and transferred into the light. You didn't have the mental capability to understand the great miracle that was occurring, and yet, you experienced it anyway.

And listen to this — there's much more that occurred in that glorious moment which you could not have fully grasped or comprehended when you called on Jesus to save you. For example, just look at the first few words of Romans 10:9, "That if thou shalt confess with thy mouth the Lord Jesus...." Put more simply, this verse says, "If you will declare Jesus is Lord...." In your confession of faith in Jesus as Lord, you removed yourself from the authority of darkness and placed yourself under the authority of the light of Christ!

The word "Lord" here, the word translated from the Greek word *kurios*, means that when you call on Jesus as Lord, you're saying, "Lord, You have the ultimate authority in my life. I'm giving you everything I am, everything I'm not, everything I will be, and everything that will ever happen to me… I'm surrendering entirely to Your lordship."

So to "confess with your mouth the Lord Jesus," as the first part of this verse states, is a confession of Jesus' lordship and your full surrender to Him.

The Two-Part Step of Receiving Salvation — an Invitation to *Everyone*

In review, the first part of Romans 10:9 says, "That if thou shalt *confess with thy mouth* the Lord Jesus…." The rest of that verse reads, "…And shalt *believe in thine heart* that God hath raised him from the dead, thou shalt be saved." Then verse 10 states, "For *with the heart man believeth* unto righteousness; and *with the mouth confession is made* unto salvation."

So we find that there are two parts to the born-again experience. First, you must believe, but it's not enough *just* to believe. There are some people who will say, "Well, I've never *confessed* my faith — I just privately believe!" According to Romans 10:10, their salvation is not complete because this verse says, "…With the mouth confession is made unto salvation." So you might *believe* Jesus is Lord in your heart, but it's when you *declare* Jesus is Lord (you declare things with your mouth) that you literally *move into salvation*.

Certainly, God sees our hearts and understands our inward thoughts toward Him. But if you can talk, simply believing Jesus is Lord without embracing Him as *your* Lord by confessing, or professing, your faith in Him falls short of the scriptural two-step instruction to both *believe* and *confess*.

What else can we learn from this passage in Romans 10? Romans 10:11 and 12 says, "For the scripture saith, Whosoever believeth on him shall not be ashamed. For there is no difference between the Jew and the Greek: for the same Lord over all is rich unto all that call upon him."

This means it doesn't matter what culture you're from, the color of your skin, or what nationality you are — *everybody gets saved the very same way!*

Verse 13 confirms that truth. It says, "For *whosoever* shall call upon the name of the Lord shall be saved."

What It *Really* Means To Be Saved — and Salvation Is a Free Gift to All Who Will Receive It

That word "saved" is a form of the Greek word *sodzo*. There's so much in that word, so much for us to partake of — to taste and see that the Lord is good. In this word "saved" there is *healing, soundness, preservation, protection, and deliverance*. All of that is contained in this word.

I want to give you an example of someone who got saved, experienced a miraculous transformation, and didn't have a clue what was taking place! I'm talking about the apostle Paul (formerly named Saul). The following is a brief account of Paul's own salvation experience.

> **And as he [Saul] journeyed, he came near Damascus: and suddenly there shined round about him a light from heaven: And he fell to the earth, and heard a voice saying unto him, Saul, Saul, why persecutest thou me?**
>
> **And he said, who art thou, *Lord*?**
>
> — Acts 9:3-5

Let's circle back to what we just read in Romans 10:13, "…Whosoever shall call upon the name of the Lord shall be saved." Paul didn't understand what he was praying. He simply called Jesus Lord, and — *bam!* — the Spirit of God inhabited him and just like that, Paul was born again.

Notice Paul didn't pray a typical religious prayer, but cried out to the Lord, asking, "Who are You, Lord?" This makes me think of my dear friend Jesse Duplantis. When Jesse got saved, he was listening to Billy Graham preach. He didn't know how to pray a prayer of repentance. He simply said to the Lord, "Lord, just do in me whatever Billy Graham just said." And *instantly*, Jesse was saved — he was born again.

Jesse made a faith confession (believing in his heart and saying with his mouth) that he was surrendering his life to the Lord. His prayer wasn't typical, but God could *see* the faith in his heart! Isn't it wonderful that God can hear our heart, and when we speak, *He can make sense out of what we're saying!*

But regardless of the exact wording he used, Jesse was born again by calling out to God when He heard the Gospel message that Jesus saves. I, too, was born again by calling on the name of the Lord. *The apostle Paul* was born again by calling Jesus Lord. And *you* were born again if you have called Jesus the Lord of your own life. Yet none of us understood the full scope of the tremendous miracle that was taking place in our lives as we called out to Jesus. But the greatest miracle of all was occurring in each of us at the moment we made Him the Lord of our lives.

Your Salvation Is an Amazing Proclamation of the Power of God!

John 1:12 says, "But as many as received him, to them gave he power to become the sons of God, even to them that believe on his name."

This verse is so packed that I want us to unpack it one piece at a time. We're going to begin with the word "but." The word "but" in Greek is the word *de* — an *exclamatory statement*. Amazingly, it's almost like John is raising his voice; he's sounding an alarm that he's about to say something totally remarkable.

The words "as many" are a form of the Greek word *hosos*, which means *as many as, as great as*, or *as much as*. It depicts *an unlimited number*. This means that, for God, there are no limitations. This verse will be true to *anyone* who calls upon the name of the Lord.

The verse says, "But as many as *received* him...." The word "received" is a form of the Greek word *lambano*. The word *lambano* means *to seize or to lay hold of something*. So you could translate this as: "As many as have seized, or laid hold of, Him...." When you seize or lay hold of something, you're doing it in order to make it your own, like a person reaching out to grab, capture, or take physical possession of something.

In many cases, this word *lambano* depicts one who graciously receives something that is freely and easily given. It is here that we begin to see a picture of salvation. God gives the call of salvation to everyone — it is both *freely* and *easily* given to us.

Salvation wasn't easy for Jesus. He died on the Cross and purchased salvation for us at a great price. *But God's grace gives salvation to us freely and easily.* The flip side of it is, *we have to seize it*. We must reach out by faith and take it. So there's a giving and there's a receiving wrapped up in this word *lambano*.

That's what happened to Rick when he was five years old. The Holy Spirit convicted his heart. The Holy Spirit did His part, but Rick had to do his part too. He had to walk the aisle. He had to reach out by faith and take what God was offering him. And regardless of the circumstances under which you became saved — whether you were in a church or not — you had to do your part to receive salvation as well.

We've looked at the words translated "but," "as many," and "received" in John 1:12. This verse goes on to say, "But as many as received him, to them *gave* he power to become the sons of God…."

The word "gave," or "give," is a form of the Greek word *didomi*, which means *to give* or *to bestow*, as a gift. Therefore, salvation is a *gift*. This word also means *to give to one who is asking*. So we know you have to *ask*.

The word *didomi* also means *to supply*. God supplies you with the authority to become a child of God! He *furnishes* it to you. And, finally, *didomi* means *to commit, to entrust, or to give into one's care*. When you put it all together, "give" means that God has entrusted and amply supplied us with what we need to be His sons and daughters. Salvation is the greatest gift we could ever receive. And when we receive it — it is our responsibility to care for it.

Your Authority and Influence in Prayer Because of Sonship

John 1:12 continues, "…To them gave he *power* to become the sons of God…." The word "power" is a form of the Greek word *exousia*, which translates as *delegated authority*. It carries the idea of influence, meaning that when you become a child of God, you immediately receive the *authority* to be a child of God. You have *influence*, particularly influence in prayer and in the spirit realm. When you become a child of God, you *instantaneously* become a person of influence.

The next words covered in that verse are "to become": "…To them gave he power *to become* the children of God…." Even the words "to become" are important. "To become" is a form of the Greek word *ginomai*. It means *to become* or *the process of becoming*. It pictures an initiated change that leads to a transition of one thing to another.

The moment you believe and confess Jesus as your Lord, you're born again. But that just *starts* the process of your walk with Him. You're going to begin growing spiritually as you transition into *full sonship* — into one who understands more and more about who he is in Christ and about his position of authority and influence as a child of God.

The word "sons" in John 1:12 is the Greek word *teknon*, which typically describes *children who are still under parental guidance at home* or *a non-adult child who remains at home and under the authority of parents*. What that means is that when you become a child of God, you move into *God's* house. In God's house, you live under the authority of God and you have influence with Him.

The verse goes on to say, "...Even to them that believe on his name...." The word "believe" here really describes a *divine impulse* or *a divine spark enabling you to believe*. Even faith in this regard is a gift (*see* Ephesians 2:8). God gives you the ability to believe on his name.

The word "on" in the Greek text is the word *eis*, which literally means *into*. It carries the idea of a merger; it depicts your entering into union with Jesus Himself. That's why we read in Romans 8:17 that we become joint-heirs with Jesus Christ — we literally enter into union or have a merger with Jesus.

The word "name" in John 1:12 is the Greek word *onoma*. The word *onoma* can depict a name, but it also depicts *a person's character*, or *a person's reputation that distinguishes him from others*. When you release your faith and believe on the name of Jesus, you enter into union, not just with the name of Jesus, with the very character — the very reputation — of Jesus Himself. A merger takes place and you become one with Him.

Your New Birth Was a Birth From Above

The words "but," "as many," "received," "gave," "power," "to become" "sons," "believe," "on," and "name" take on new brand-new meaning when you understand all that is packed into that one verse! And they are especially meaningful when you read John 1:12 together with verse 13:

> **But as many as received him, to them gave he power to become the sons of God, even to them that believe on his name: which were born, not of blood, nor of the will of the flesh, nor of the will of man, but of God.**

You see, this new birth was given to you by God. It's what Jesus referred to in John 3:7 when He said to Nicodemus, "...Ye must be born again."

Interestingly, in the Greek text, it says "You must be born from above." To be born from above is a divine birth, and according to John 1:13, it is not of blood, it is not of the will of the flesh, and it is not of the will of man — *but it is a birth which comes to you OF GOD when you are born again.*

At that moment, you experience the greatest miracle that can ever take place. Immediately, you become *a partaker of divine sonship* — you become a son of God. You come under the light of Christ and under His authority — and you have delegated authority from Him. *And you move into God's house.*

When you were first saved, you probably didn't understand all this. The understanding of what happened in your new birth, when you became a son or daughter of God, is something you'll have to grow in as you spend time in His Word and really begin to "taste and see that the Lord is good"!

STUDY QUESTIONS

Study to shew thyself approved unto God, a workman that needeth not to be ashamed, rightly dividing the word of truth.
— 2 Timothy 2:15

1. What are the two elements of receiving salvation according to Romans 10:9 and 10? What corresponding action must accompany your believing in God and His Word in order to receive from Him? (*See* Mark 11:23 for help understanding this connection.)
2. What is the Greek word that describes our receiving from God what He so graciously gives? Take time to write out its meaning. Can God's gift of eternal salvation be received independently of this word? Why or why not?
3. If you are born again, did you honestly understand the fullness of what occurred at the moment of your new birth? What did you learn in this lesson about *divine sonship* that was granted to you immediately when you received Jesus as your Lord?

PRACTICAL APPLICATION

But be ye doers of the word, and not hearers only, deceiving your own selves.
—James 1:22

1. What do you remember most about the time when you called on the name of the Lord for salvation? Take time to rehearse that miraculous moment and either write it down or tell it to a friend or loved one.
2. In the program, Rick expounded on several words from the Greek in John 1:12 — "but," "as many," "received," "gave," "power," "to become," "sons," "believe," "on," and "name." Write down the word that ministered most to you and why.
3. Meditate on the correlation between coming under Christ's authority in the new birth and your God-given ability to exercise spiritual authority as you submit to Christ and His Word. Can you articulate the connection between the two? (Consider James 4:7 to help formulate your response.)

LESSON 2

TOPIC
We Are Partakers of the Divine Nature

SCRIPTURES

1. **Psalm 34:8** — O taste and see that the Lord is good: blessed is the man that trusteth in him.
2. **John 1:12** — But as many received him, to them gave he power to become the sons of God, even to them that believe on his name.
3. **John 1:13** — Which were born, not of blood, nor of the will of the flesh, nor of the will of man, but of God.
4. **2 Peter 1:2** — Grace and peace be multiplied unto you through the knowledge of God, and of Jesus our Lord.
5. **2 Peter 1:3** — According as his divine power hath given unto us all things that pertain unto life and godliness, through the knowledge of him that hath called us to glory and virtue.
6. **2 Peter 1:4** — Whereby are given unto us exceeding great and precious promises: that by these ye might be partakers of the divine nature....

GREEK WORDS

1. "through" — ἐν (*en*): in, as in the sphere where an act occurs; by, as in the agency by which an act occurs
2. "knowledge" — ἐπίγνωσις (*epignosis*): a compound of the preposition ἐπί (*epi*) and the word γινώσκω (*ginosko*); ἐπί (*epi*) is used as an intensifier, and γινώσκω (*ginosko*) is interpreted as the idea of knowing; it means I know, I perceive, I realize, or I recognize; when compounded, the terms form the word ἐπίγνωσις (*epignosis*), meaning experiential, firsthand, and personal knowledge, or one who is on top of his subject
3. "divine power" — θείας δυνάμεως (*theias dunameos*): the word θείας (*theias*) always describes that which is divine as opposed to that which is human, or ordinary; the word δυνάμεως (*dunameos*), a form of the Greek word *dunamis*, denotes explosive, superhuman power that comes with enormous energy and produces phenomenal, extraordinary, and unparalleled results; *dunamis* depicts mighty deeds that are incomparable and beyond human ability to perform; miraculous powers or manifestations; a force of nature comparable to a hurricane, tornado, or earthquake; the full force of an advancing army
4. "given" — δίδωμι (*didomi*): to give or to bestow as a gift; to give to one who is asking; to supply or furnish; to commit, entrust, or to give into one's care
5. "unto us" — ἡμῖν (*hemin*): meaning directly to us
6. "all things" — τὰ πάντα (*ta panta*): the word πάντα (*panta*) means everything; the definite article τὰ (*ta*) is used to add force; not *just* things, but *so many* things
7. "pertain" — πρός (*pros*): relating to or touching
8. "life" — ζωὴν (*zoen*): natural life; a life that is lived with gusto and zest
9. "godliness" — εὐσέβεια (*eusebeia*): a compound of the preposition εὖ (*eu*) and σέβομαι (*sebomai*); the preposition εὖ (*eu*) means good, well, or swell and speaks of something that is wonderful; the word σέβομαι (*sebomai*) pictures what one esteems, reverences, or worships; compounded as εὐσέβεια (*eusebeia*), it speaks of an individual's deep sense of devotion, godliness, piety, and reverence
10. "through" — διά (*dia*): can be translated by, as in the agency by which it occurs, or through, as in the instrument through which an event occurs

11. "hath called" — καλέω (*kaleo*): to beckon, call, invite, or summon; conveys the idea of those called or invited to an event that is normally closed to the public; an invitation to attend; an event that can only be attended by those with a VIP invitation
12. "to" — ἰδίᾳ (*idia*): by his own personal power; refers to God's initiative and power to carry it out
13. "glory" — δόξα (*doxa*): not power, but glory; the word δόξα (*doxa*) means the radiance or splendor of God, but also speaks of the weightiness of God's presence
14. "virtue" — ἀρετή (*arete*): excellence; related to the term ἄρρην (*arren*), which refers to manliness, but likely from αἴρω (*airo*), which means "I lift"; as the word ἄρρην (*arren*) it pictures the strength to lift something up; as ἀρετή (*arete*), it pictures one's excellent strength; here, a picture of God's mighty, muscular ability to lift one from a place of destruction to a place of sonship
15. "whereby" — δι' ὧν (*di hon*): through which; showing the instrumentality by which promises were provided; that is, God's glory and excellence provided the following
16. "exceeding great and precious" — τὰ τίμια καὶ μέγιστα (*ta timia kai megista*): the word τίμια (*timia*) means dear, honored, or of great price; μέγιστα (*megista*) translates to great, as in something so great that words are not adequate to describe it; the definite article τὰ (*ta*) adds force and intensity; together, the translation depicts that which is dear, honored, precious, valued, and so magnificent that words cannot express it
17. "promises" — ἐπάγγελμα (*epangelma*): plural form of the word promise; thus, many promises
18. "that" — ἵνα (*hina*): points to the ultimate effect of these promises
19. "by" — διά (*dia*): depicts agency or instrumentality; by them or through them
20. "partaker" — κοινωνός (*koinonos*): sharers or partakers; something commonly shared and possessed; joint participation; used to denote things like marriage, a family sharing life together, or a joint family property; here, it refers to a divine nature which is commonly shared between Christ and His people
21. "divine" — Θείας (*theias*): a form of θεῖος (*theios*); denotes that which is divine

22. "nature" — φύσις (*phusis*): nature, as in human nature; as such, it refers to the instinctive behaviors and characteristics that accompany human nature; but here, it is the divine nature and refers to the instinctive behaviors and characteristics that accompany a divine nature

SYNOPSIS

In order to understand Psalm 34:8 and truly "taste and see" that the Lord is good, one must *partake* of the blessings made available to us upon the moment of our salvation. In order to partake of His *divine nature*, we must learn what salvation has afforded us in Christ. In this lesson, you will learn about the many things the Lord has given us and about the part we play in actively receiving these blessings as we grow and walk with God.

The emphasis of this lesson:

It's a wonderful thing to be born again! We know from our previous lesson how to receive salvation and partake of divine sonship, but how do we then begin partaking of His divine nature? From the moment we were saved, God gives us the promise of *all things* **(***see* **2 Peter 1:3). By "all things," God wants to give us the ability to transform our unrenewed mind and fleshly nature into the divine nature. To undergo such a transformation beyond the new birth, we must aspire to an expert knowledge of Him. It is through this knowledge that we see that God has given us great and precious promises. Once we understand this, God's gifts of grace, peace, power, and virtue are released to operate as a reality in our lives.**

We're told in Second Peter 1:4, "Whereby are given unto us exceeding great and precious promises: that by these ye might be partakers of the divine nature…" In our last lesson, we learned that when we're born again, we *literally* become the sons of God. Our status of sonship allows us to partake of the blessings made available to us upon our salvation. God wants us to experience the full extent of His blessings. In today's lesson, we will discover what great and precious promises He has given us, and how by these promises we can become active *partakers of the divine nature*.

Our theme verse, Psalm 34:8, says, "O taste and see that the Lord is good…." The Lord is good, and He wants us to "taste" and see how good He is. The verse goes on to say, "…Blessed is the man that trusteth in

Him." The word "trust" has to do with faith, which means **when you exercise your trust in the Lord,** *that's when you unlock how good and sweet He is.*

In the last lesson, we saw in John 1:12,13 that the Bible says, "But as many as received Him, to them gave He the power to become the sons of God, even to them that believe on His name: which were born, not of blood, nor the will of the flesh, nor the will of man, but of God."

In John 3:3, Jesus told Nicodemus that a man must be born again — *born of God*. In the Greek, Jesus says a man must be *born from above*. To be born from above is a heavenly birth in which God literally gives us the ability to become the children of God.

The following is an abbreviated version of Rick Renner's testimony of being born again, or *born from above*:

> I experienced such a heavenly birth when I was just five years old. I'd been under conviction of sin and of my need for Jesus as my Savior, and, finally, after a year, I walked the aisle to answer the altar call. I went down to the front of the church — right onto the altar, and took the hand of my pastor, Brother Post. He said, "Ricky, why have you come?"
>
> I said, "Brother Post, I've come today to give my heart and my life to Jesus." Because I was so young, they sent me over to the front pew where I waited for my Sunday School teacher, named Jerry. And when Jerry came, he and I got on our knees together, and he asked me a series of questions to make sure I really understood what I was doing by giving my life to Jesus. I then asked Jesus to come into my heart and declared Him to be the Lord of my life.
>
> When I finished, I looked to my side and my parents had come out of the choir loft to join me. So when I stood up to make my public proclamation of faith, my mother and my daddy were standing there with me. During the evening service, I was water-baptized, and that day began my spiritual life as a born-again believer. I was five years old, and I really didn't have clue what happened inside me, except that I had given my life to Jesus.

Most people don't know what happens when they get saved, and that's why we must learn about the transformation that comes with salvation.

Our Knowledge of God — and How It Releases His Grace and Peace Into Our Lives

Second Peter 1:2 says, "Grace and peace be multiplied unto you…" *How would you like for grace and peace to be multiplied to you?* This word "grace" describes *a touch of God that empowers you* to do things you couldn't do alone, or by yourself. The word "peace" here refers to *the cessation of war*, to reconstruction, and to *a time of rebuilding peace and prosperity in your life. Who wouldn't want to have grace and peace to be multiplied unto them so they could experience this supernatural empowering touch and the reconstruction of peace and prosperity in their lives?*

"Multiplied" in this verse means *to be multiplied repeatedly*, like a cascading effect that never ends. Since grace and peace are supposed to be continuously multiplied to you, the longer you serve the Lord, the more of this "cascading blessing" you should experience.

You may ask, "*How can grace and peace be multiplied to me in this way?*" Second Peter 1:2 says it's "through the knowledge of God, and of Jesus our Lord."

You must *learn* in order for His grace and peace to be multiplied to you. When the Bible says "through the knowledge," this word "through" is the Greek word *en*, which can be translated as *in the knowledge*, or this knowledge can depict *the agency by which all these blessings come to you*. Therefore, we find that grace and peace are multiplied to us through or by the knowledge of God and Jesus our Lord. Knowledge opens the floodgates for us. That's why we must learn what happened to us when we became saved.

The word "knowledge" in this phrase "through the knowledge" is the Greek word *epignosis*. It's a compound of the preposition *epi* and the word *ginosko*. The preposition *epi* in this word is used as an intensifier. It pictures *one who is on top of his subject*. The word *ginosko* carries the idea of *knowing something*. It means *I know, I perceive, I realize*, and *I recognize*. Simply put, *epi* means *to be on top of* and *ginosko* means *to know*. But when you compound the two words, it forms the Greek word *epignósis*, which pictures *experiential knowledge, firsthand knowledge*, and *personal knowledge*.

To be on top of your knowledge means it is *expert* knowledge. God doesn't want us to stop until we have attained expert knowledge about God and the Lord Jesus Christ. And the more knowledge we gain, the more grace and peace cascade into our lives.

Our Knowledge of God Releases Divine Power

Let's return to Second Peter 1. From verse 2 we know that as we cultivate an expert knowledge of the Lord, His grace and peace flow abundantly in our lives. But what else does this knowledge release? Peter continues in verse 3, "According as his divine power hath given unto us all things that pertain unto life and godliness…."

You may wonder, *I know that being saved guarantees me a place in Heaven, but what about all these things that pertain to life and godliness in this life?* From this verse, we know that salvation guarantees us more than the promise of Heaven. When God promises us "all things," He really means *all things*! And according to the rest of Second Peter 1:3, the "all things" God is promising come to us *through the knowledge of Him who called us to glory and virtue*.

Let's take a moment to unpack this verse word by word, beginning with the words "divine power." This term "divine power" in the Greek is *theias dunameos*. The first word *theias* always refers to that which is *divine*, as opposed to that which is human or ordinary. The second word *dunameos* is a form of the Greek word *dunamis*, and it denotes *power* — but not just *any* power. It's *an explosive, superhuman power that comes with enormous energy and produces phenomenal, extraordinary, and unparalleled results*.

This word *dunamis* also depicts *mighty deeds that are impressive, incomparable and beyond human ability to perform* — miraculous powers or manifestations. It is also the same word used to describe *a force of nature, such as a hurricane, tornado, or an earthquake*.

Lastly, this word *dunamis* was also the word used by the Greeks and the Romans to describe *the full might of an advancing army*. And in this verse, it is connected to the word *theias*, the word for "divine," which means when we became saved, divine power — superhuman, extraordinary power beyond our imagination — was released into our lives. It is a "mighty deed" kind of power — power that shakes things up like a hurricane, tornado, or earthquake. And this power of God was so mighty that when it was released into us in the new birth, it was like the army of God or a raging storm that cannot be harnessed as it began pushing darkness out of our life. When this power is active and operative in us — *wow!* — it gives us something that we could never otherwise possess on our own.

God's Divine Power Is a Precious Gift — and Here's How We Ought To Use It

What does His divine power give us? Going back to the beginning of Second Peter 1:3, we read, "According as his divine power hath given unto us all things…." But first, let's focus on the word "given," a form of the Greek word *didomi*, which means *to give*, or *to bestow as a gift — to give to one who is asking*. Divine power is available to us as a gift the moment we get saved. To receive this precious gift, *we must ask in order to receive.*

This word *didomi* also means *to supply* or *to furnish*. Therefore, when God gives us this power, He fully supplies it to us, and we are fully furnished with it. It also means *to commit*, *to entrust*, or *to give into one's care*. Notice that in this verse, Peter used this word in the past tense. He was describing what has already happened — the moment you got saved, *this amazing power was literally given to you as a gift!* And when it was entrusted to you, it fully supplied you, fully furnished you, and was placed into your care. Divine power is a precious gift that we have been entrusted to care for, which means we've been charged to use it and develop it.

Next, Peter added the words "unto us." These words are of great importance; in the Greek "unto us" is the word *hemin*, which means *directly to us*. Make no mistake — divine power is what God has given directly to us! There are no hoops to jump through and no qualifications or certifications we can present in order to receive this gift "unto us." Once we make our proclamation of faith in the Lord Jesus Christ, *we are direct recipients of His divine power!*

God's Power Has Made 'All Things' Available to Us — But It's the Pursuit of Knowledge That Opens the Floodgates

Verse 3 continues to say, "…As his divine power hath given unto us *all things* that pertain to life and godliness…." Let's start with the Greek meaning of "all things," which is *ta panta*.

The word *panta* comes from *pan*, meaning *everything*. The word *ta* connected to *pan* also means everything, but the little *ta* in front of *panta* is a definite article that is meant to add force to the statement. It's not just *things*, but *so many things*. In verse 3, Peter is saying that God's divine power has given unto us *an abundance of things* that pertain unto life and godliness.

Next, we reach the word "pertain." The word "pertain" is the Greek word *pros*, and here it means *relating to* or *touching* life and godliness. The word "life" is the word *zoen*, which describes life, as in natural life, but it also depicts *a life that is filled with gusto and zest*. From the very moment you receive salvation, boredom is supposed to leave your life.

God has given us everything we need *relating to* or *touching* life — the life that we're leading right now — and godliness. The word "godliness" used here describes *everything that we need to be good, godly people*. All of that has been given to us. In fact, verse three says *how* it has been given to us: "through the knowledge of him that hath called us to glory and virtue."

If you're saved, you have all these things, but many people are not aware of these blessings. That's why you need to gain knowledge. From what we've read in verse two, we know that grace and peace cascade to us and are multiplied in our lives *through the knowledge of God and the Lord Jesus Christ*. And in verse three, we find that God's divine power has given everything to us *relating to* or *touching* life and godliness. This, too, is released in us *through the knowledge of him that has called us to glory and virtue*.

Therefore, studying your Bible and utilizing tools like this study guide are crucial in your walk with the Lord. In doing these things, you are gaining knowledge, *a knowledge that opens the floodgates for all this to operate in your life.*

This word "through" in verse three is the word *dia*, which means *through the agency of*, or *through the instrumentality of*. We find that all these good things are released in our lives through the *agency*, or *instrumentality* of the knowledge of the Word of God.

The Call to Salvation Is a VIP Invitation From God

Continuing in Second Peter 1:3, we learn that we have been given all things that pertain to life and godliness "…through the knowledge of him that hath *called* us to glory and virtue."

The word "called" in the Greek is the word *kaleo*, meaning *I call*. It also means *to beckon, to call, to invite*, or *to summon*. It means we've been *personally invited* — *WOW!* We've been called, we've been invited, and we've been summoned by the Lord God Himself!

This word *kaleo* was also used to convey the idea of *those called or invited to an event that was normally closed to the public*. In other words, you couldn't come unless you were invited. You could only participate in such an event if you have received a VIP invitation — *and that's what the Gospel message is*. It's a VIP invitation to come to Christ, to reconciliation with God, to the family of God, and to eternal salvation.

In history, this word *kaleo* was used to describe royal events that were normally closed to the public. A person couldn't attend without being invited, and receiving an invitation to attend this type of special occasion was a great honor to be treasured, prized, and revered. Therefore, *it is really a big deal that you're saved*. God issued you a VIP invitation through His Spirit, and you accepted the invitation and came to Christ. This is why Jesus said in the gospel of John that *no man can come unto the Father except the Holy Spirit draws him* (*see* John 6:44). If you're saved, it's because through the Gospel message, God gave you a VIP invitation — you could never have been saved without it.

When God extends a call for someone to be saved, one needs to understand that *God Himself is opening that person's heart to receive and his ears to hear* — *He is giving that individual the ability to answer the call!*

God's Personal Power Lifts Us From a Place of Darkness

Second Peter 1:3 continues, "… Of him that hath *called* us to glory and virtue."

Here we find a mistake in the Greek text. In the *King James Version*, it says, "…Of him that hath called us to glory and virtue," as we already read. However, in the Greek it says, "He has called us by His own power and virtue." And "His own (personal) power" is referring to God's power to carry out something. But "power" is also a bad translation because in Greek, "power" in this phrase is the word *doxa*, which is not power, but *glory*.

He has called us to glory, power, and virtue. The word "virtue" comes from the Greek word *arete*, which describes *excellence*. It is also related to another Greek word *arren*, which refers to *manliness*. Let's take a moment to explore this. Likely derived from the word *airo*, which means *I lift*, this word *arren* pictures *the strength of a man* or *a muscular person*. In this context, we can see that *arete* pictures *one's excellent strength*.

When you combine these meanings in the context of Second Peter 1:3, it depicts a picture of *God's mighty, muscular ability to lift one from a place of destruction into a place of sonship.* That is simply amazing!

God gives you the VIP invitation, puts forth all His abilities to lift you out of a place of destruction, and places you in His family as a son or daughter. All of that happened the moment you got saved.

Salvation Gives Us the Birthright To Become Partakers of the Divine Nature

Second Peter 1:4 states, "Whereby are given unto us exceeding great and precious promises: that by these ye might be partakers of the divine nature…." *Exceeding great and precious promises* sounds wonderful, but what does that mean? In Greek, the phrase "exceeding great and precious promises" is *ta timia kai megista*. The word *timia* means *dear, honored, of a great price, precious*, and *valued*. The word *megista* means *great* — as in something *so great, words are not adequate to describe it*. Peter was talking about precious promises. Notice that "promises" is plural, meaning that God hasn't given us *one*, but He's given us *many*. And by these *many* promises, *we can become partakers of the divine nature*. We can truly "taste and see that the Lord is good" (*see* Psalm 34:8)!

The word "partaker" is the Greek word *koinonos*, which means *something in common that is shared and possessed* — a joint participation. For example, it's used to denote a marriage shared between two people, a family that shares their lives together, or joint family property. And in Second Peter 1:4, it describes *divine nature that is commonly shared between Christ and His people*. That makes us joint participants of the divine nature with the Lord Jesus Christ!

The word "divine" depicts *that which is divine*. And the word "nature" is the Greek word *phusis*, which describes *nature*, like human nature and all the behaviors that are normally instinctive of human nature. In this case, it's describing *divine nature*, which means that upon your salvation, *you have the divine nature, and everything instinctive about divine nature is working inside of you!*

Just like humans are instinctual and do certain things, the divine nature of God has its own instinctual characteristics. As you gain more knowledge about the Word of God, the knowledge of God, and the knowledge of the Lord Jesus Christ, *divine nature begins to operate inside you*. All of these things the Lord our God has promised us and has made available to us by His personal invitation to us to receive salvation. It is by our pursuit of knowledge and growth as people who are born again that we can begin to identify His divine nature operating in our lives!

STUDY QUESTIONS

> **Study to shew thyself approved unto God, a workman that needeth not to be ashamed, rightly dividing the word of truth.**
> **— 2 Timothy 2:15**

1. According to Second Peter 1:2-4, God gives us everything we need pertaining to life and godliness. How has God given us these things? What must we do to access these precious gifts?
2. What are a few ways you can develop an expert knowledge of the Lord?
3. Take a moment to write the Greek transliteration and meaning of the word "partaker." What does it mean to be a partaker? Describe how this meaning parallels our relationship with the Lord when we become *partakers of His divine nature*.

PRACTICAL APPLICATION

> **But be ye doers of the word, and not hearers only, deceiving your own selves.**
> **— James 1:22**

1. In Second Peter 1:3, God's "divine power" is described as an explosive, superhuman power that comes with enormous energy and produces phenomenal, unparalleled results. It also describes the power of God to push out the darkness in our lives like an advancing army. Have you ever experienced this divine power in your life? Describe a time when you witnessed the divine power of God.
2. Second Peter 1:4 tells us that God wants us to be partakers of the divine nature. What are some characteristics of His divine nature that you see operating inside you and in your life? In what areas of your life do you want to see God's divine nature operate more?

LESSON 3

TOPIC
We Are Partakers of Divine Deliverance

SCRIPTURES
1. **Psalm 34:8** — O taste and see that the Lord is good: blessed is the man that trusteth in him.
2. **2 Peter 1:3** — According as his divine power hath given unto us all things that pertain unto life and godliness, through the knowledge of him that hath called us to glory and virtue.
3. **2 Peter 1:4** — Whereby are given unto us exceeding great and precious promises: that by these ye might be partakers of the divine nature....
4. **Colossians 1:13** — Who hath delivered us from the power of darkness, and hath translated us into the kingdom of his dear Son....
5. **Ephesians 1:7** — In whom we have redemption through his blood, the forgiveness of sins, according to the riches of his grace.

GREEK WORDS
1. "to" — ἰδίᾳ (*idia*): by His own personal power; refers to God's initiative and power to carry it out
2. "virtue" — ἀρετή (*arete*): excellence; related to the word ἄρρην (*arren*), which refers to manliness, but likely from αἴρω (*airo*), which means "I lift"; as the word ἄρρην (*arren*), it pictures the strength to lift up; as ἀρετή (*arete*), it pictures one's excellent strength; here, we find a picture of God's mighty, muscular ability to lift one from a place of destruction to a place of sonship
3. "given" — δίδωμι (*didomi*): to give; to bestow as a gift; to give to one who is asking; also means to supply, to furnish, to commit, to entrust, or to give into one's care; here, it is past tense: "has given"
4. "unto us" — ἡμῖν (*hemin*): to us; no mistake, these have been given directly to us

5. "exceeding great and precious" — τὰ τίμια καὶ μέγιστα (*ta timia kai megista*): the word τίμια (*timia*) means dear, honored, of great price, precious, and valued, while μέγιστα (*megista*) means great, as in something so great that words are not adequate to describe it; the definite article τὰ (*ta*) adds force; here, we find the phrase to mean dear, honored, precious, valued, and so magnificent that words cannot adequately express it
6. "promises" — ἐπάγγελμα (*epangelma*): plural form of the word promise; thus, many promises
7. "that" — ἵνα (*hina*): points to the ultimate effect of these promises
8. "by" — διά (*dia*): depicts agency or instrumentality; by them or through them
9. "partakers" — κοινωνός (*koinonos*): sharers or partakers; something commonly shared and possessed; joint participation; used to denote marriage, family, or joint family property; here, a divine nature that is commonly shared between Christ and His people
10. "divine" — Θείας (*theias*): a form of θεῖος (*theios*); denotes that which is divine
11. "nature" — φύσις (*phusis*): nature, as in human nature; as such, it refers to the instinctive behaviors and characteristics that accompany human nature; but here, it is the divine nature and refers to the instinctive behaviors and characteristics that accompany a divine nature
12. "delivered" — ῥύομαι (*rhuomai*): to rescue; to snatch from danger; to deliver; depicts removing someone from danger or oppression; to snatch just in the nick of time
13. "from" — ἐκ (*ek*): out; from; exit
14. "power" — ἐξουσία (*exousia*): authority, control, dominion, influence, or power
15. "darkness" — σκότος (*skotos*): darkness and everything connected with darkness
16. "translated" — μεθίστημι (*methistimi*): to transfer from one place to another place
17. "we have" — ἔχομεν (*echoed*): we have, hold, and possess
18. "redemption" — ἀπολύτρωσις (*apolutrosis*): to be released by a payment; to purchase back again; specifically used for purchasing a slave out of the slave market

19. "through" — διά (*dia*): can be translated by, as in the agency by which it occurred, or through, as in the instrument through which this event took place
20. "forgiveness" — ἀφίημι (*aphiemi*): to forgive; to permanently dismiss; to release; to set free; to let go; to discharge; to send away; to liberate completely; to forfeit one's right to ever bring it up again; used in New Testament times in reference to canceling a debt or releasing someone from the obligation of a contact, a commitment, or a promise; to forfeit any right to hold a person captive to a previous commitment or wrong he has committed; to irretrievably remove
21. "according to" — κατά (*kata*): a preposition that can be translated according to, but importantly carries the sense of a dominating and subjugating force; hence, it pictures being dominated and subjugated by something

SYNOPSIS

God has called us to "taste," or experience, the goodness of the Lord. The Lord is so good, and He has given us all things. God Himself initiated the glorious plan of salvation into our lives through His divine power, so that we may partake of His exceedingly great and precious promises. However, God's promises are locked up, and it is only when we begin to study the Word of God and dive deep into understanding the promises of God that they begin to cascade into our lives. It is through exercising our faith and seeking out the knowledge of Him that we truly become partakers of His divine promises.

Prior to our salvation, we were living in darkness — swallowed up in the will of Satan. Our nature was one of rebellion and our life was a life of bondage and captivity. But according to God's divine power, He has delivered us from this life of bondage and darkness. Because of His sacrifice, the blood of Jesus has set us free. We have been forgiven — our nature transformed from worldly to divine. God removed us from the enemy's domain, and His mighty power enabled us to exit from the power of darkness. When God put forth His mighty power, He lifted us from a place of bondage and destruction into a place of Sonship. This act is divine deliverance.

The emphasis of this lesson:

God's mighty, muscular power has lifted us from a place of bondage into the Kingdom of His dear Son. This is *divine deliverance*. When Jesus came to earth, He was sent on a divine rescue mission to remove us from the enemy's domain. Before our salvation, we were living under the dominion, control, and authority of darkness. But God made a way for us — He removed us from darkness and everything having to do with darkness. And when we exited the power of darkness, we entered into the favor of God. It was by the blood of Jesus that we were afforded redemption from sin and bondage. Through the blood of the Lamb, we were transformed and our sinful, rebellious nature was traded for His divine nature — we were made completely different and new. And by His divine nature we became partakers of divine deliverance.

In today's lesson, we will dissect what it means to be partakers of *divine deliverance*. Let's begin with our theme verse Psalm 34:8, which says, "O taste and see that the Lord is good: blessed is the man that trusteth in him." The Lord is so good, and we are to "taste" Him — to *experience* Him. We experience the Lord's goodness with trust and faith.

That word "trusteth" has to do with faith. If you want to taste and see that the Lord is good, you must use your faith — *your faith will unlock the goodness of God in your life*!

In our last lesson, we covered Second Peter 1:3 and 4. Verse 3 reads, "According as his divine power hath given unto us all things that pertain unto life and godliness…." The phrase "all things" in Greek is *ta panta*. The word *ta* refers to *many things*, and the word *pan* is all-inclusive. The word *ta* at the end also means *many things*. When you put these meanings together, *ta panta* refers to *what things*, *how many things*, or *oh so many things* have been given unto us by God that pertain unto life and godliness.

The word "pertain" in Greek is the word *pros*. A better translation would be that God has given unto us all things that *touch* life and godliness — all things that *have to do with* life and godliness. It is here we find that God's promises are not just about heaven. He has given us *everything — so many things*! What an incredible list of things God has given us that pertain to life and godliness!

That word "life" in Greek is the word *zoen*. It refers to *physical life* and *a life filled with gusto and zest*. This means that God really wants you to have an abundant life, and He's given you everything you need to have an abundant life. The rest of Second Peter 1:3 tells us *how* we experience these things. It says, "…through the knowledge of him that hath called us to glory (power) and virtue."

From the two previous lessons, we know that God gave us many promises at the moment of our salvation, but we also know that we must put forth our own effort to truly receive the abundance of His promises. All of God's promises are "locked up," but as you open the door and begin to study the Word of God and dive deep, all of the promises of God and everything He has provided for life and godliness will begin to cascade into your life.

God Has Called Us to 'Glory' and 'Virtue'

Now, let's shift our focus today to the final portion of Second Peter 1:3, specifically He who hath called us to glory and virtue. It says, "According as his divine power hath given unto us all things that pertain unto life and godliness, through the knowledge of him that hath called us *to glory and virtue*."

The word "to" in Greek is *idia*. In the context of our scripture, *idia* describes God who has called us *by His own personal power*. It refers to God's initiative and power to carry it all out. God Himself initiated the glorious plan of salvation in our lives, and He alone has the power to carry it out. And notice verse 3 says, "…to glory and *virtue*."

Let's take a closer look at this word "virtue." "Virtue" is the Greek word *arete*, which describes *excellence*. But it's also related to the word *arren*, which refers to *having the quality of manliness*. You might be thinking — *What does this have to do with God?* Well, it's likely derived from the word *airo*, which means *to lift*. As the word *arren*, "virtue" pictures the strength to lift something up; as *arete*, it pictures one's excellent strength. In Second Peter 1:3, we find that "virtue" signifies a picture of *God's mighty, muscular ability to lift one from a place of destruction to a place of sonship*.

God's mighty, muscular power was involved in your salvation. He put forth His excellence and His virtue in order to raise you from that desolate place of destruction and then to elevate you to a place of divine sonship. It is this holy process that we call *divine deliverance*.

Second Peter 1:4 begins, "Whereby are given unto us exceeding great and precious promises…." The word "given" is a form of the Greek word *didomi*, which means *to give, to bestow as a gift*, or *to give to one who is asking*. This tells us we must be asking and actively seeking out these gifts from God. And if you ask, God will bestow it unto you as a gift — *because He gives to those who are asking*.

In addition, the word *didomi* also means *to supply, to fully furnish, to commit, to entrust*, or *to give into one's care*. And here it is past tense, which means God has already given and made available to us *all of His great and precious promises*! He has entrusted them to us, and He has given them into our care. All of this is referred to in the past tense, which means that this *actually* happened when Jesus died for us on the Cross, and the day — the very moment — we said "yes" to the lordship of Jesus Christ, it became a reality in our lives.

This verse reiterates that God has given these promises "unto us"; there's no mistaking it. The words "unto us" in Greek literally mean *directly to us*. And not just directly to someone else or to someone who has had a strong relationship with the Lord for ages — *this verse is talking to you*! This direct gift is not conditional. Once you receive the gift of salvation, God places these things directly into your care.

God's Amazing Gift —
Exceeding Great and Precious Promises!

So what has the Lord given us? Second Peter 1:4 says He has given us *exceeding great and precious promises*.

The phrase "exceeding great and precious promises" in Greek is the definite article *ta* combined with the words *timia* and *megista*. The word *timia* means *dear, honored*, and *of a great price* — to be precious and valued. *Megista* depicts something *great*, as in *something so great that words are not adequate to describe it*. The use of the definite article *ta* adds force to its accompanying phrase. Therefore, as we read our verse in the text, we find that it pictures *dear, honored*, and *valued* promises, *so magnificent* that words cannot describe them. These are the promises God has given to us — *what God has already given to you!*

> **Whereby are given unto us exceeding great and precious promises: that by these ye might be partakers of the divine nature....**
> **— 2 Peter 1:4**

Notice that the word "promises" is plural here, meaning *many promises*. God has given us so many promises — and He has given them to us so that by them, we might become partakers of the divine nature. The word "that" is the Greek word *hina*, which points to a conclusion or the ultimate effect of these promises. "Partakers" is a form of the Greek word *koinonos*. It describes those who are *sharers and partakers* or *something that is commonly shared and possessed*. It depicts a marriage, family, or joint family property. In the text, it pictures a divine nature that is commonly shared between Christ and His people.

In our last lesson, we learned about the importance of this divine nature. To review, "divine" in Greek is the word *theias*, which denotes *that which is divine* as opposed to that which is human. The word "nature" here is the Greek word *phusis*, referring to the word *nature*, as in *human nature*. Normally, it would depict the distinctive behaviors and characteristics that accompany human nature, but here it's describing a divine nature that was given to us in our new birth, meaning that within us we possess this divine nature.

We're partakers of the divine nature. And we've seen in Second Peter 1:3 and 4 that God put forth His own personal power to lift us out of the place of bondage and destruction into a place of sonship — that is our *divine deliverance*.

God's Divine Rescue Mission of Deliverance

The apostle Paul described this moment of divine deliverance in Colossians 1:13. It reads, "Who hath delivered us from the power of darkness, and hath translated us into the kingdom of his dear Son." This verse is packed with insights into our topic of divine deliverance.

The word "delivered" in Greek is the word *rhuomai*, meaning *to rescue* or *to snatch up from danger*. In this context, it could be translated *He has rescued us* or *He has snatched us from danger* and literally means to deliver or rescue someone from danger or oppression, or to snatch someone just in the nick of time. This tells us that when Jesus came to earth, He came on a divine rescue mission to snatch us out of the enemy's domain. He removed us from darkness — *and He did so just in the nick of time*!

Verse 13 goes on to say God has delivered us *from* the power of darkness. This word "from" is the Greek word *ek*, which means *out of* or *from*. It's where we get the word for an exit. So, the power of God has enabled us to *exit* the power of darkness. The word "power" here is the Greek word *exousia*. It describes *authority, control, dominion, influence*, and *power*, which means before we got saved, we were under the authority, control, dominion, influence, and power of darkness — but God's power made a way for us to exit the power of darkness.

The word "darkness" is the Greek word *skotos*, which refers to *darkness and everything connected to darkness*. According to this scripture, God's power made a way for us to *literally* exit from the power of darkness and everything connected with it. When God's power removed us from this darkness, we entered into God's Kingdom instead. *Glory to God!*

The Lord is so good — He delivered us out of darkness and translated us into the Kingdom of His dear Son. This word "translated" comes from the Greek word *methistimi*, meaning *to leave one place and then enter into a brand-new place*. This perfectly describes what God's divine deliverance has done for us.

Redemption Through the Blood of Jesus Christ

When we received salvation and called Jesus the Lord of our life, God's power literally made an exit for us out of the control of darkness and into His Kingdom. It was *through the blood of Jesus* that you were removed from the power of darkness and placed into the Kingdom of God. Ephesians 1:7 says, "In whom we have redemption through his blood, the forgiveness of sins, according to the riches of his grace."

The words "we have" are a translation of the Greek word *echomen*. It comes from the word *echo* and means *we have, we hold*, or *we possess*. In other words, it is in Jesus that *we have, we hold*, and *we possess* redemption. "Redemption" in Greek is the word *apolutrosis*, meaning *to be released by a payment* or *to purchase back again*. Specifically, this term was used for purchasing a slave out of the slave market.

In this program, Rick reads an excerpt from his book *Dressed to Kill* to provide a closer look at what the slave market was like at the time the apostle Paul wrote this verse. The following is an excerpt:

The slave market was dreadful and deplorable place. Such places should have never been permitted. Human beings were paraded in front of potential buyers and were then placed on the trading block where they were auctioned off like animals, old furniture, or unwanted junk.

The slaves' value was determined primarily by the condition of their teeth. If they had good teeth, they were probably in good shape and were therefore more expensive. If they had rotten teeth, they probably could be bought rather cheaply.

So before the nauseating process of buying, selling, and trading human debris began, potential buyers were allowed to check out the "merchandise." The slaves' heads were shoved up and backwards; their mouths were forcibly jerked opened; and their teeth were inspected to see if they were rotten or in fairly good shape.

As if this wasn't inhumane and degrading enough, slave-buying customers were also encouraged to kick and hit the "merchandise" in order to determine the slaves' level of physical fitness.

To discover the slaves' temperament, buyers slapped them, cursed at them, and spat in their faces. If a slave could swallow his pride, grit his teeth, and hold his temper during such humiliating abuse, the buyer assumed he could be used to the point of abuse without giving his owner any kind of trouble.

In short, slaves had no personal worth. They were viewed to be no better than animals. According to the thinking of the day, they were just another kind of workhorse and had no real human value. Their only purpose in the world was to serve the demands that their current owners exacted of them.

Like slaves in the slave market, we stood helpless before the devil as he slapped our lives around — hitting us, kicking us, spitting upon us, and abusing us in every way he possibly could. Our "slaveowner" tried to damage our self-image, kill our bodies with various kinds of sin and vices, and mar us emotionally. When he was finished using one form of bondage and death on us, he would place us back on the trading block to be auctioned off again. Soon another form of bondage would overtake us and begin to make its own destructive marks on our lives.

Thus, we were passed from one bondage to the next in a never-ending cycle of defeat. Each day we lived, whether we were aware of it or not, this hellish ownership took us further downward and ever deeper into the captivity of sin and total depravity — lock, stock, and barrel, from the inside out, from the beginning to the end, every inch from head to toe, backward and forward, and up to the brim.[1]

This means that prior to our salvation, we were swallowed up in the will of Satan. Our prior slavery to the devil was so deeply seeded in us that our nature became intrinsically meshed together with the seed of rebellion, which is at the very core of Satan's nature. Rebellion against God ran *so deep* in our blood and became *so ingrained* in our human disposition, that eventually the gulf between God and us was *vast*. Scripture declares that we even became alienated and enemies in our minds through wicked works (*see* Colossians 1:21).

But according to Ephesians 1:7, that's not who we are now. The verse says, "In whom we have redemption…." Jesus has set us free from the bondage of slavery. We have been purchased out of Satan's hideous slave market through Jesus' blood shed for us on the Cross.

The word "through" in Greek is the word *dia*. It describes *the agency or instrumentality by which our deliverance took place*. It was through the agency and instrumentality of the blood of Jesus that we received the forgiveness of our sins. The word "forgiveness" is so wonderful — there's so much more in this word than people realize. In Greek it is the word *aphiemi*, which means *to forgive, to permanently dismiss, to release completely, to set free or let go, to discharge, to send away*, or *to liberate forever*. It also means *to forfeit one's right to ever bring something up again*. In the New Testament, "forgiveness" is used in reference to cancelling a debt or releasing someone from the obligation of a contract, commitment, or a promise. It can also mean *to forfeit any right to hold a person captive to a previous commitment or wrong that they may have committed* or *to irretrievably remove*. Under the blood of Jesus, God has *irretrievably removed* every sin you have ever committed so that you can be a partaker of His divine deliverance.

In Conclusion

In review, Ephesians 1:7 tells us, "In whom we have redemption through his blood, the forgiveness of sins, according to the riches of his grace." The term "according to" is the Greek word *kata*. It is a preposition that can be translated as *according to*, but it also carries the idea of being dominated or subjugated by something. In this scripture, we find that we're dominated by the riches of God's grace. This is what happens when we receive *divine deliverance*!

God intends for us to be partakers of this divine deliverance and to enjoy our new freedom and life that He has given us. Jesus came into the world, which was Satan's slave market, and He saw us on the auction block. He paid the price of our redemption with His own blood, and He *delivered* us. He snatched us out of darkness just in the nick of time.

It was through the blood of Jesus that God enabled us to make an exit from that slave market — out from the power of darkness. And once we left the control and dominion of darkness, we were translated into the Kingdom of God. It was through a great sacrifice that this truly divine deliverance was made available to us, and God intends for us to partake of and to enjoy our freedom and our deliverance.

STUDY QUESTIONS

> **Study to shew thyself approved unto God, a workman that needeth not to be ashamed, rightly dividing the word of truth.**
> **— 2 Timothy 2:15**

1. What does the word "delivered" mean in Colossians 1:13? How does this impact your view of what took place at the moment of your salvation?
2. What does it mean to be "translated" into the Kingdom of God (*see* Colossians 1:13)?
3. Why are the words "we have" important in Ephesians 1:7? What do they tell us about the reality of our redemption through the blood of Jesus?

PRACTICAL APPLICATION

> But be ye doers of the word, and not hearers only, deceiving your own selves.
> —James 1:22

1. Our divine deliverance took place through the precious blood of Jesus that was shed for us on the Cross. What have you learned from this lesson that has shaped your view of what really took place when Jesus delivered you out of darkness?
2. Refer back to the passage Rick read from *Dressed To Kill* in this lesson. What does this tell you about where Jesus purchased you from and where you are today?
3. What kind of life has God called us to? Review Second Peter 1:3 and 4 and reflect on the divine realities God wants you to experience now in this life.

---

[1]Rick Renner, *Dressed To Kill: A Biblical Approach to Spiritual Warfare and Armor* (Shippensburg, PA: Harrison House Publishers, 1991), pp. 81-82,84.

LESSON 4

TOPIC

We Are Partakers of Divine Healing

SCRIPTURES

1. **Psalm 34:8** — O taste and see that the Lord is good: blessed is the man that trusteth in him.
2. **2 Peter 1:3** — According as his divine power hath given unto us all things that pertain unto life and godliness, through the knowledge of him that hath called us to glory and virtue.
3. **2 Peter 1:4** — Whereby are given unto us exceeding great and precious promises: that by these ye might be partakers of the divine nature....

4. **1 Peter 2:24** — Who his own self bare our sins in his own body on the tree, that we, being dead to sins, should live unto righteousness: by whose stripes ye were healed.
5. **Isaiah 52:14** — As many were astonied at thee; his visage was so marred more than any man, and his form more than the sons of men.
6. **Psalm 107:20** — He sent his word, and healed them, and delivered them from their destructions.

GREEK WORDS

1. "to" — ἰδίᾳ (*idia*): by his own personal power; refers to God's initiative and power to carry it out
2. "virtue" — ἀρετή (*arete*): excellence; related to the word ἄρρην (*arren*), which refers to manliness, but likely from αἴρω (*airo*), which means "I lift"; as the word ἄρρην (*arren*), it pictures the strength to lift up; as ἀρετή (*arete*), it pictures one's excellent strength; here, we find a picture of God's mighty, muscular ability to lift one from a place of destruction to a place of sonship
3. "given" — δίδωμι (*didomi*): to give; to bestow as a gift; to give to one asking; also means to supply, to furnish, to commit, to entrust, or to give into one's care; here, it is past tense, "has given"
4. "unto us" — ἡμῖν (*hemin*): to us; no mistake, these have been given directly to us
5. "exceeding great and precious" — τὰ τίμια καὶ μέγιστα (*ta timia kai megista*): the definite article τὰ (*ta*) with τίμια (*timia*) and μέγιστα (*megista*); the word τίμια (*timia*) means dear, honored, of great price, precious, and valued, while μέγιστα (*megista*) means great, as in something so great that words are not adequate to describe it; the definite article τὰ (*ta*) adds force; here, we find it to mean dear, honored, precious, valued, and so magnificent that words cannot adequately express it
6. "promises" — ἐπάγγελμα (*epangelma*): plural form of the word promise; thus, many promises
7. "that" — ἵνα (*hina*): points to the ultimate effect of these promises
8. "by" — διά (*dia*): depicts agency or instrumentality; by them or through them
9. "partakers" — κοινωνός (*koinonos*): sharers or partakers; something commonly shared and possessed; joint participation; used to denote

marriage, family, or joint family property; here, a divine nature that is commonly shared between Christ and His people

10. "divine" — Θείας (*theias*): a form of θεῖος (*theios*); denotes that which is divine

11. "nature" — φύσις (*phusis*): nature, as in human nature; as such, it refers to the instinctive behaviors and characteristics that accompany human nature; **but here**, it is the divine nature and refers to the instinctive behaviors and characteristics that accompany a divine nature

12. "bare" — ἀναφέρω (*anaphero*): to bear up or to lift up; pictures high priests in a temple whose responsibilities were to offer physical sacrifices upon an altar

13. "our sins" — τὰς ἁμαρτίας ἡμῶν (*tas hamartias hemon*): the sins of us, our own sins; points to the truth that this sacrifice was for us

14. "in" — ἐν (*en*): literally means *in*, and emphatically means Christ bare our sin *in* His own body on the Cross

15. "own body" — τῷ σώματι αὐτοῦ (*to somati autou*): literally translated in the body of Him, or in His own body

16. "on" — ἐπὶ (*epi*): upon; it designates the place where this final sacrifice occurred

17. "tree" — τὸ ξύλον (*to zulon*): depicts what is made of wood, but especially used to depict the crossbeam on which a victim hung when he was crucified; it can be translated tree, but in fact, depicts the Cross

18. "that" — ἵνα (*hina*): points expressly to the purpose of Christ's sacrifice

19. "dead" — ἀπογίνομαι (*apoginomai*): a compound of the preposition ἀπο (*apo*) and the word γίνομαι (*ginomai*); the preposition ἀπο (*apo*) means away and carries the idea of separation, and the word γίνομαι (*ginomai*) means to become or to emerge; compounded, the word ἀπογίνομαι (*apoginomai*) means to be separated away from sin and to emerge from it as something entirely different and new

20. "live" — ζάω (*zao*): depicts that which is alive or lively as opposed to what is lifeless or dead, but also carries the idea of a life filled with gusto and zest

21. "righteousness" — δικαιοσύνη (*dikaiosune*): derived from δίκη (*dike*), it pictures a judicial verdict of one fully examined who is found either not guilty or to have no guilt; thus, righteous and approved; in the

New Testament, it depicts the righteousness of God, or the approval that God gives to those who are deemed to be right with Him or righteous
22. "stripes" — **μώλωψ** (*molops*): a full-body bruise; refers to a terrible lashing that draws blood and produces discoloration and swelling of the entire body
23. "healed" — **ἰάομαι** (*iaomai*): a well-known word used throughout the four gospels to describe certain aspects of Jesus' healing ministry; it means to cure or to be doctored, and often denotes healing power that progressively reverses a condition; due to its progressive nature, it is often translated as a treatment or a remedy; borrowed from the medical world to describe the physical healing or curing of the human body, and in the New Testament gospels (where it is used regularly) it is only used in connection with physical and mental healing

SYNOPSIS

Similar to how we can use our faith and seek out the knowledge of God to unlock His many promises, we must also understand what divine healing is and how it was afforded to us in order to receive the fullness of it. We must realize that Christ not only acted as the Lamb of God who shed His blood for the forgiveness of our sins, but He also acted as the high priest preparing the holy sacrifice of His body on the Cross. It wasn't just any crucifixion but *the* Crucifixion — *the* Cross, unlike any other cross. It became the great altar on which the blood of the Lamb was shed and where the permanent forgiveness of our own sins was procured. Because of the Cross, when we received salvation, our sins were forgiven, our debts were cancelled, and our old nature died to give place to God's divine nature — and we emerged from it as something different and brand new. We have been spiritually transformed from death to life in Christ! Jesus paid the penalty for our sins with His own body, and the stripes laid across His body paid the price for our healing.

The emphasis of this lesson:

The Lord is infinitely good, and His desire is for us to partake of Him and all the riches of His glory. God has *a lot* to give us. One of the things the Lord wants us to partake of is *divine healing*. The Bible tells us in Second Peter 1:4 that God has given us great promises, and by these promises we can become partakers of the divine nature. And part

of God's divine nature that He wants us to partake of is His divine healing.

Psalm 34:8 tells us, "O taste and see that the Lord is good: blessed is the man that trusteth in him." We know that the Lord is good, but what exactly does it mean to "taste and see?" It means that the Lord wants us to experience the fullness of His goodness and blessings — He wants us to witness their abundance as they cascade into our life. But *how* do we experience these things? Verse 8 tells us that "blessed is the man that *trusteth* in Him." That word "trusteth" can also be translated as "faith"; therefore, the goodness of God is released *by our faith*.

God has *so many* good things for us. Second Peter 1:3 says, "According as his divine power hath given unto us all things that pertain unto life and godliness…." Praise God that we have the promise of Heaven, but we need God's promises in our day-to-day life as well. This verse tells us that God has given us all things that "pertain" to both life and godliness. In the Greek, it actually says everything *touching* life. And the word "life" describes *physical life* — the life that we are living right now through the knowledge of Him who has called us to glory and virtue.

According as his divine power hath given unto us all things that pertain unto life and godliness, through the knowledge of him that hath called us to glory and virtue.
— 2 Peter 1:3

Notice the words "through the knowledge." This tells us that we need to gain knowledge of the promises of God. As these promises become known to you and you begin to unlock them, you become a partaker in all the wonderful promises God has provided for us.

Verse 3 continues, "…through the knowledge of him that hath called us *to* glory and virtue." The word "to" in Greek is the word *idia*, which literally means *by His own personal power*. It refers to God's initiative and His power to carry it all out. God starts this work in our life, and He alone has the power to carry it out to fulfillment. And what has He called us to? He has called us to glory and virtue.

As we learned in previous lessons, the word "virtue" is the Greek word *arete*, meaning *excellence*. It's also related to the Greek words *arren* and *airo*. The word *arren* refers to *manliness*, and *airo* means *I lift*. But the word *arete*, as Peter used it in this verse, "virtue" pictures God's *mighty, muscular ability to lift one from a place of destruction to a place of sonship.* It shows God putting forth His great arm to snatch us out of danger just in the nick of time. That is divine deliverance.

Second Peter 1:4 also tells us, "Whereby are given *unto* us exceeding great and precious promises...." The words "unto us" are a translation of the Greek word *hemin*. This word means there is no mistaking it, these things have been given *directly to us.*

Verse 4 continues, "Whereby are given unto us *exceeding great and precious promises*...." When this is read in Greek, the sentence structure is very important to its meaning. It translates to the phrase *ta timia kai megista.* It is comprised of the definite article *ta* and the words *timia* and *megista.* The word *timia* depicts that which is *dear, honored,* and *of great price* — something precious and highly valued. The word *megista* means *great,* as in *something so great that words are not adequate to describe it.*

The definite article *ta* also adds force; so here the complete phrase depicts that which is *dear, honored, precious, valued,* and *so magnificent that words simply cannot express its significance.* With this phrase, Peter was referring to the significance of the great and exceeding promises of God — promises that are so magnificent, so dear, that they can't even be described or expressed. It's important to note that this was not just one promise, but multiple promises.

God has given us an abundance of promises, but why did He give them? So that we might become "partakers" of the divine nature (*see* 2 Peter 1:4). The word "partakers" is the Greek word *koinonos,* which means *a sharer* or *a partaker.* It depicts *something commonly shared and possessed* or *joint participation.* It was used to denote a marriage, family, or joint family property. In verse 4, "partakers" pictures the divine nature that is commonly shared between Christ and His people, meaning we really participate in the divine nature of Christ.

Divine Healing Is Part of the Lord's Divine Nature

We've seen that in Second Peter 1:4 the word "divine" is the Greek word *theias,* and it denotes *that which is divine.* "Nature" is the word *phusis,* which normally describes human nature and all the characteristics that are instinctive of that nature. But here it isn't describing human nature — it's describing *the divine nature of Christ.* This means that when Christ came into you through the power of the Holy Spirit at the moment of your salvation, you received a new nature — a divine nature. You became a participant in the nature of God, and now you have been equipped with everything that is characteristic and instinctive of His divine nature — *amazing!*

One aspect of God's divine nature that He wants us to participate in is *divine healing*. In other words, we are to be partakers of divine healing. First Peter 2:24 says, "Who his own self bare our sins in his own body on the tree, that we, being dead to sins, should live unto righteousness: by whose stripes ye were healed."

In the program, Rick shared that he was raised in a particular denomination that put great importance on teaching the Bible but did not necessarily believe that healing was the will of God. And when they came to First Peter 2:24, "…by whose stripes ye were healed," it was taken to mean that we were spiritually healed the day we got saved. But in fact, nobody gets spiritually healed the day they're saved. Before we received salvation — *we were dead*. And you can't heal a dead person. Then, the day we got saved, we were quickened to life and made alive again. You were not healed but *raised from spiritual death*.

Jesus Paid the Ultimate Price So That We May Partake of Divine Healing

The word "healed" used in First Peter 2:24 always describes physical healing. According to this verse, just like Jesus bare our sins in His own body on the tree, Jesus with His stripes paid the price for us to be physically well.

Let's breakdown this verse in the Greek. It begins, "Who his own self bare our sins in his own body on the tree…." The word "bare" is the Greek word *anaphero*, which means *to bare up* or *to lift up*. It pictures priests in a temple whose responsibilities were to offer physical sacrifices upon the altar. Here we find that Christ was not only the Lamb of God whose blood was shed for the forgiveness of sin, but in that moment, He was simultaneously the high priest who offered His own blood on the altar of the Cross.

As the high priest, Jesus was lifting up His own holy blood, and the Bible says He bare our *sins*. "Sins" in the Greek points to the truth that this sacrifice was for us, for *the sins of us* or *our own sins*. It was not just for someone else but for *our sins*. And First Peter 2:24 says Jesus "bare our sins *in* his own body on the tree." The word "in" is the Greek word *en*, which literally means *in*. It is not symbolic language — it means that Christ literally bare our sin *in* His physical body. He bore it *in* Himself. It also emphasizes that God transferred sin and all of its accompanying effects into the body of Jesus as He hung on the Cross.

Verse 24 continues, "Who his own self bare our sins in his *own body* on the tree...." The words "own body" in Greek literally says *in the body of Him* or *in His own body* on the tree. The word "on" is the Greek word *epi*, meaning *upon*, and it designates the place where this final sacrifice for our sins and our physical healing occurred. The word "tree" has a definite article before it, and it is significant. In Greek, *to zulon* depicts *anything that is made out of wood*. But it was especially used to depict the cross beam on which a victim hung when he was crucified. So it could be translated "tree" as we see in this verse, but more accurately, this term depicts the Cross. The reason the definite article is so important is because there were many Roman crucifixions. By using the definite article here, Peter was reminding us that this was not just any old crucifixion, it was *the* Crucifixion — *the Cross unlike any other cross*.

In that moment, the Cross became the great altar upon which Christ's blood was shed and the permanent forgiveness of sin was procured for all who come to faith in Him. Jesus was (and is) the high priest who offered His life as a sacrifice, and the Cross was the altar.

First Peter 2:24 goes on to say, "...that we, being dead to sins, should live unto righteousness...." The word "that" is the Greek word *hina*, and it is a pointer word, meaning it points toward the reason for or the purpose of Christ's sacrifice. The word "dead" is the Greek word *apoginomai*, a compound of the preposition *apo* and the word *ginomai*. The preposition *apo* means *away* and carries the idea of separation. The word *ginomai* means *to become* or, in this case, *to emerge*. But when compounded, this word translates to mean *to be separated away from sin and emerged from it as something entirely different and new*. That is what happened because of the Cross. When we made Jesus the Lord of our life by confessing Him as Lord, in that moment our sin was forgiven, our debt was cancelled, and our old "man," or old nature, died. We emerged from it as something different and new.

Then, First Peter 2:24 tells us, "...that we, being dead to sins, should *live* unto righteousness...." The word "live" is the Greek word *zao*, which depicts *that which is alive or lively*. It describes a life that is *filled* with gusto and zest. This means that when you come to Christ, your life is not supposed to be boring! It is meant to be *lively*, to be filled with gusto and zest — *that* is God's plan for you. And because you are a partaker of God's divine nature, you should be experiencing that kind of life. That is why you need knowledge (*see* 2 Peter 1:3). This life and these promises come to us through the knowledge of God and Jesus.

In Christ we are no longer spiritually dead but *alive unto God*! We're filled with gusto and zest so we might live unto righteousness. The word "righteousness" is the Greek word *dikaiosune*. This word is derived from the word *dike*, which depicts *a judicial verdict of one who is not found guilty and, therefore, is approved and righteous*. We no longer have to walk around like we're guilty and still bound in sin. God has declared us right, He's declared us approved, and He's declared us *righteous*!

The Cross and Stripes of Jesus — A Holy Remedy

At the end of First Peter 2:24, Peter adds, "…By whose stripes ye were healed." The word "stripes" here is important; although, it is poorly translated in most Bible translations. In Greek, it is the word *molops*, and it describes *a full-body bruise*. It would be better translated, "by His full body bruise." It's describing what happened to Jesus during His scourging and His duration on the Cross. Specifically, it refers to the terrible lashing that draws blood and produces discoloration and swelling of the entire body. It also means that in addition to the stripes that were laid across Jesus' body by those who scourged and beat Him, His body was completely swollen, disfigured, and discolored from the physical abuse that He endured. The scourging that Jesus experienced so disfigured His body that Isaiah 52:14 describes it like this:

> **As many were astonied at thee; his visage was so marred more than any man, and his form more than the sons of men.**

That is how disfigured His body was and that is what the word "stripes" means in this verse — to be completely disfigured, to be swollen from all of the beating one has received. But the Bible says that because of Jesus' swollen body — by His stripes — "ye were healed" (1 Peter 2:24). The word "healed" is a well-known word, used especially throughout the four gospels to describe certain elements of Jesus' physical healing ministry. It means *to cure* or *to be doctored*, and it often denotes a healing power that progressively reverses a condition. It's often translated as the word "remedy," which means that the Cross and those stripes on Jesus' body were the remedy for your physical healing. This means God *really* brought healing to you through these symbols of Jesus' great sacrifice.

In the New Testament, this word for "healing" is always used in connection with physical or mental healing. So Peter's declaration that the wounds laid across Christ's body were for the healing of every believer, describes *you*. And because he wrote it in past tense, it emphatically means your healing was purchased on the Cross and is a right given to every child of God!

The Cross and those stripes on Jesus' body were God's remedy and cure for sickness. The particular form of the word which Peter used conveys a *completed action done in the past*. It is a done deal, and now you can claim it by faith!

It shouldn't surprise us that God has always been in the healing business. For example, Psalm 107:20 says:

> **He sent his word, and healed them, and delivered them from their destructions.**

There's no doubt that divine healing is a part of God's divine nature that He wants us to partake of. As we've seen, First Peter 2:24 confirms this. Christ paid the penalty for our sin in His own body on the Cross as our great high priest. He lifted up His own blood to atone for our sins, and with the stripes that were laid across His body, Jesus fully and completely paid the price for our healing.

From this we can be confident that exceeding great and precious promises have been given to us and that we may be partakers of *everything* Christ procured for us on the Cross. By seeking out the knowledge of the Lord God, we see such promises — divine sonship, divine nature, divine deliverance, and divine healing — and take them by faith.

STUDY QUESTIONS

> Study to shew thyself approved unto God, a workman that needeth not to be ashamed, rightly dividing the word of truth.
> — 2 Timothy 2:15

1. Why can we be certain First Peter 2:24 does not simply refer to spiritual healing? What have we learned about the state we were in before being born again that confirms this?
2. First Peter 2:24 says Jesus "bare" our sins in His body on the Cross. What is significant about this word? What does it tell us about the role Jesus had on the Cross?
3. The *King James Version* translates the end of First Peter 2:24 as "by whose stripes ye were healed." Why is this a bad translation of the word "stripes"? What would be a better translation of this word?

PRACTICAL APPLICATION

> But be ye doers of the word, and not hearers only, deceiving your own selves.
> —James 1:22

1. Second Peter 1:4 says we are to partake of God's divine nature, which includes healing. Have you ever experienced divine healing in your life? If so, take a moment to share your experience.
2. First Peter 2:24 tells us that because of Jesus' sacrifice we have not only died to sin, but we have been given the ability to *live unto righteousness*. Are you living a rich life that is filled with gusto and zest? Why or why not?
3. The word for "healing" used in First Peter 2:24 means *to cure* or *to be doctored* and is always used to refer to physical or mental healing in the New Testament. This verse tells us that the Cross and the stripes on Jesus' body really were the remedy for your physical healing. Take a moment to pray for any physical healing that is needed in your life or in the lives of those you know.

LESSON 5

TOPIC
We Are Partakers of Divine Provision

SCRIPTURES
1. **Psalm 34:8** — O taste and see that the Lord is good: blessed is the man that trusteth in him.
2. **2 Peter 1:3** — According as his divine power hath given unto us all things that pertain unto life and godliness, through the knowledge of him that hath called us to glory and virtue.
3. **2 Peter 1:4** — Whereby are given unto us exceeding great and precious promises: that by these ye might be partakers of the divine nature....
4. **Romans 8:16** — The Spirit itself beareth witness with our spirit, that we are the children of God.
5. **Romans 8:17** — And if children, then heirs; heirs of God, and joint-heirs with Christ....
6. **John 16:14** — He shall glorify me: for he [the Holy Spirit] shall receive of mine, and shall shew it unto you.
7. **John 16:15** — All things that the Father hath are mine: therefore said I, that he shall take of mine, and shall shew it unto you.
8. **Philippians 4:19** — But my God shall supply all your need according to his riches in glory by Christ Jesus.

GREEK WORDS
1. "to" — ἰδίᾳ (*idia*): by his own personal power; refers to God's initiative and power to carry it out
2. "virtue" — ἀρετή (*arete*): excellence; related to the word ἄρρην (*arren*), which refers to manliness, but likely from αἴρω (*airo*), which means "I lift"; as the word ἄρρην (*arren*), it pictures the strength to lift up; as ἀρετή (*arete*), it pictures one's excellent strength; here, we find a picture of God's mighty, muscular ability to lift one from a place of destruction to a place of sonship

3. "given" — **δίδωμι** (*didomi*): to give; to bestow as a gift; to give to one asking; also means to supply, to furnish, to commit, to entrust, or to give into one's care; here, it is past tense, "has given"
4. "unto us" — **ἡμῖν** (*hemin*): to us; no mistake, these have been given directly to us
5. "exceeding great and precious" — **τὰ τίμια καὶ μέγιστα** (*ta timia kai megista*): the definite article **τὰ** (*ta*) with **τίμια** (*timia*) and **μέγιστα** (*megista*); the word **τίμια** (*timia*) means dear, honored, of great price, precious, and valued, while **μέγιστα** (*megista*) means great, as in something so great that words are not adequate to describe it; the definite article **τὰ** (*ta*) adds force; here, we find it to mean dear, honored, precious, valued, and so magnificent that words cannot adequately express it
6. "promises" — **ἐπάγγελμα** (*epangelma*): plural form of the word promise; thus, many promises
7. "that" — **ἵνα** (*hina*): points to the ultimate effect of these promises
8. "by" — **διά** (*dia*): depicts agency or instrumentality; by them or through them
9. "partakers" — **κοινωνός** (*koinonos*): sharers or partakers; something commonly shared and possessed; joint participation; used to denote marriage, family, or joint family property; here, a divine nature that is commonly shared between Christ and His people
10. "divine" — **Θείας** (*theias*): a form of **θεῖος** (*theios*); denotes that which is divine
11. "nature" — **φύσις** (*phusis*): nature, as in human nature; as such, it refers to the instinctive behaviors and characteristics that accompany human nature; **but here**, it is the divine nature and refers to the instinctive behaviors and characteristics that accompany a divine nature
12. "beareth witness with" — **συμμαρτυρέω** (*summartureo*): a compound of the preposition **σύν** (*sun*) and the word **μαρτυρέω** (*martureo*); the preposition **σύν** (*sun*) means to do something jointly or together and carries the idea of partnership; the word **μαρτυρέω** (*martureo*) means to attest, to give evidence, to testify, or to witness; as a compound, it shows the work of the Spirit to attest, to give evidence, to testify, or to witness with our own human spirit that we are the children of God
13. "our spirits" — **τῷ πνεύματι ἡμῶν** (*to pneumati hemon*): literally the spirit of us; our own spirits

14. "that" — ὅτι (*hoti*): specifically that
15. "we are" — ἐσμὲν (*esmen*): not becoming, but presently are
16. "children" — τέκνα (*tekna*): children under parental guidance at home; one who remains under the authority of parents; it is most widely used to describe children who are under parental guidance
17. "and" — δέ (*de*): intended to make a dramatic and strong point
18. "if" — εἰ (*ei*): if; as the case actually is
19. "heirs" — κληρονόμος (*kleronomos*): an inheritance; an heir; a lot cast in one's favor; thus, to hit the jackpot in terms of an inheritance
20. "heirs of God" — μὲν Θεοῦ (*men Theou*)
21. "joint-heirs" — συγκληρονόμος (*sunkleronomos*): a compound of the preposition σύν (*sun*) and κληρονόμος (*kleronomos*); the preposition σύν (*sun*) means to do something jointly or together with and carries the idea of partnership; the word κληρονόμος (*kleronomos*) means an inheritance, and it portrays an heir or a lot cast in one's favor, thus, to hit the jackpot in terms of an inheritance; as "joint heirs" it means we are equal heirs with Jesus Christ in everything He has inherited from the Father
22. "shew" — ἀναγγέλλω (*anangello*): to announce, disclose, divulge, proclaim, or relate
23. "unto you" — ὑμῖν (*humin*): directly to you
24. "but" — δέ (*de*): intended to make a dramatic and strong point
25. "supply" — πληρόω (*pleroo*): to fill completely; filled to the point of overflowing satisfaction
26. "all" — πᾶσαν (*pasan*): all; all-encompassing, leaving nothing out
27. "needs" — χρείαν (*chreian*): plural form of χρεία; business, deficits, needs, necessities, or wants
28. "according to" — κατά (*kata*): a preposition that can be translated according to, but importantly carries the sense of a dominating and subjugating force; hence, it pictures being dominated and subjugated by something
29. "riches" — πλοῦτος (*ploutos*): immense wealth or riches beyond imagination; many riches; pictures one who possess wealth so immense that is it immeasurable; abundant riches or measureless resources

SYNOPSIS

The Lord has given us exceeding great and precious promises, and we are to partake of them by faith and through the knowledge of our Lord Jesus Christ. We must trust and know that these divine promises belong to us — they were inherited by us the moment we were saved. When we become children of God, we enter into the house of the Lord, and in that very instant the Holy Spirit begins to minister to us. He discloses, divulges, and proclaims directly to us what belongs to us as joint heirs with Christ Jesus. It is through this status as an heir and this inheritance that we are to partake of God's divine provisions.

The emphasis of this lesson:

By the salvation afforded to us by God's mighty power, we have become the heirs of God and joint heirs with Christ Jesus. We have been given access to the greatest inheritance there is — a wealth that is vast and immeasurable. This means that everything that belongs to Jesus belongs to us as the children of God. The Holy Spirit proclaims to us through His work that God has supplied *all* our needs. His provision is one that fills to the point of overflowing satisfaction and supplies all our needs, leaving nothing out.

The Bible tells us in Second Peter 1:4 that God has given us promises. And by these promises, we can *literally* be partakers of the divine nature. Part of what we are to partake of is *divine provision*. In Lesson 1 we learned about what actually happened to us the day we got saved. In Lesson 2, we saw that God wants us to partake of His divine nature and that He has given us exceeding great and precious promises. In Lesson 3, we learned that God wants us to be partakers of divine deliverance through the blood of Jesus. And in the previous lesson, we discovered that Jesus bare our sins in His body on the Cross and endured a brutal scourging for us to walk in divine healing — and by His stripes, or His full-body bruise, we are healed. In this lesson, we will learn what it means to be a partaker of *divine provision*.

To begin, let's review our theme verse Psalm 34:8, which says, "O taste and see that the Lord is good: blessed is the man that trusteth in him." When we trust in God and use our faith, we begin to appropriate all His goodness.

Second Peter 1:3 reads, "According as his divine power hath given unto us all things that pertain unto life and to godliness...." In the Greek, "unto us" is *directly to us*, and "all things" means *everything* — nothing left out that pertains to life and godliness. The word "pertain" in Greek is the word *pros*. Translated this means that God has given us everything, *absolutely everything*, relating to or touching life. The word "life," is the Greek word *zoe*, and refers to not just heavenly life but life right now — *physical life*. And "godliness" means that God wants for us to have a *good, godly* life.

How do we activate all of these things in our lives? The Bible says through the knowledge of Him that has called us to glory and virtue (*see* 2 Peter 1:3). We must have knowledge of what the Lord has provided for us because we can only enter into these promises if we know that they belong to us.

God's Divine Promises — And How We Become Partakers of Them!

The word "virtue" is the Greek word *arete*. This word is related to the word *arren*, which carries the idea of *manliness* or *the strength of a man*. It's likely also a derivative form of the Greek word *airo*, which means *to lift up*. As *arete*, it pictures *one's excellent strength*, but in the context of Second Peter 1:3, we find that it pictures God's mighty, muscular ability to reach into the world and grab ahold of us, to take us from a place of destruction, to snatch us from danger, and to elevate us to a higher place — *a place of sonship*. It took the mighty power of God to lift us out of that place of sin to where we are now!

Continuing in Second Peter 1:4, it says, "Whereby are given unto us exceeding great and precious promises: that by these ye might be partakers of the divine nature...." The word "given" is a form of the Greek word *didomi*, meaning *to bestow* or *to give as a gift* — to give to one who is asking. It also means *to supply or fully furnish* or *to commit, entrust,* or *give into one's care*. In verse four, "given" is past tense, which means in the past God completely gave to us — He bestowed as a gift and He entrusted into our care — exceeding great and precious promises. He gave us these promises because we asked. God gave them to us as a gift, and because "given" also means *to give into one's care*, we have a responsibility to care for them — to maintain them and exercise them. He has given us the gift of these exceeding great and precious promises so that by them, we might become partakers of His divine nature — *amazing!*

The words "exceeding great and precious" literally mean that these promises are *dear, honored, precious, valued*, and *so magnificent* that words simply cannot express how marvelous they are. The word "promises" is also plural in verse four, which means that God hasn't just given us one or a few — He has given us *so many* promises, that by these we might be partakers of the divine nature.

The word "that" in the Greek is the word *hina*. It points to the reason why these promises were given: *in order that* we might be partakers, or *in order that by these promises* we might be partakers. The word "by" is the Greek word *dia*, which carries the idea of agency or instrumentality: *by these* or *through these*. And that's why verse four says "that by these" — or through these promises — we might become partakers of the divine nature.

The word "partakers" is a form of the Greek word *koinonos*, which refers to *a sharer* or *a partaker*. It describes *something commonly shared and commonly possessed* or where there is *joint participation*. It can also denote marriage, because marriage is shared; or family, because family is shared; or a joint family property that's owned by everybody in the family. Here, it describes the divine nature that is commonly shared between Christ and His people. You may wonder, what do you mean by *divine nature*? The word "divine," the Greek word *theias*, describes *that which is divine* as opposed to that which is natural or human. The word "nature" is the Greek word *phusis*, which is the word you would use to describe something that does something naturally, like *human nature*.

It is human nature to do certain things. For example, when fish are born from their eggs, they immediately begin to swim. You don't have to give a fish swimming lessons; they begin swimming immediately. Why? Because they're fish, and it is their *nature* to swim. In the same way, we were given a new, divine nature in our new birth.

We're not who we used to be — we are new. We died to sin and have emerged as something completely different and new. We have received a divine nature, and we are to be partakers of it.

And just like a fish swims because it is a fish, there are certain things we ought to do. There are certain things we ought to possess simply because we have a divine nature. One of the things that belongs to us by inheritance is *divine provision*. That is the focus of this lesson. We all have needs — we all need provision — and God has provided so much for us.

The Great Inheritance of God's Divine Provision

Romans 8:16 says, "The Spirit itself beareth witness with our spirit, that we are the children of God." Notice the *King James Version* says the Spirit *itself*. The Holy Spirit is not an *it*; the Holy Spirit is a *Him*. He's the third member of the Trinity. The Greek actually says *autos*, or the Spirit *himself*. It's referring to the personality of the Holy Spirit. You could read Romans 8:16:

> **The Spirit *Himself* beareth witness with our spirit, that we are the children of God.**

What does it mean when the Bible says the Spirit beareth witness with our spirit? "Beareth witness" is the Greek word *summartureo*, a compound of the preposition *sun* and the word *martureo*. The preposition *sun* means *to do something jointly* or *to do something with*. It carries the idea of a partnership. The word *martureo* means *to attest*, *to give evidence*, *to testify*, or *to witness*. When you compound these words together, it shows that the work of the Spirit is *to attest*, *to give evidence*, *to testify*, or *to witness* with our own spirit that we are the children of God.

When you called Jesus the Lord of your life and became born again, immediately the Holy Spirit inside you began to witness to you. He started working with you so that you would know you are a child of God. And notice the verse says, "The Spirit itself beareth witness with *our spirit*...." The Greek literally says *the spirit of us* or *our own spirits*. The moment you were saved the Holy Spirit began to witness to your spirit that you are a child of God.

Verse 16 continues, "The Spirit itself beareth witness with our spirit, that we are the children of God." The word "that" in Greek is the word *hoti*, meaning *specifically that*. And importantly, the words "we are" are a translation of the Greek word *esmen*, which states that we are not becoming children of God, *we already are, right now, in this very moment*. The word "children" is a form of the Greek word *tekna*, which depicts *children under parental guidance at home* or *a child who remains under the authority of his or her parents*. In the context of Romans 8:16, it means the Spirit bears witness to us that we have moved in and have become part of the family of God — *we're living in God's house!*

When we're born again, we don't have to wonder about our identity because it is the Holy Spirit's job to *immediately* begin to attest and witness to us — to give us evidence — that we are the children of God.

In Romans 8:17, Paul added, "And if children, then heirs; heirs of God, and joint-heirs with Christ…." The word "and" in Greek is the word *de*; it is a conjunction intended to make a dramatic and strong point. It is the equivalent of saying, "Listen to this!" The word "if" is the Greek word *ei*, which means *if* — or *as the case actually is*. So in this verse, Paul was saying, "If, as the case is, we become children, children of God living in God's house, then we also become heirs — heirs of God and joint heirs with Christ."

The word "heirs," the Greek word *kleronomos*, depicts *an inheritance*. Here, it depicts an heir, but it can also describe a lot that's been cast in one's favor, which means the moment we were placed in Christ, a lot was cast in our favor. In other words, we have hit that jackpot in terms of an inheritance. People today are playing the lottery all the time hoping they can win the big jackpot. Well, the truth is that the moment we were born again, the lot was cast in our favor and we did hit the jackpot. So what do we become heirs of? According to verse 18, we become *heirs of God*.

The Greek says "men found." This word "men" is *emphatic* — it is categorical and unmistakable — and it literally means that if, as the case is, we moved into God's house, we have now become His children, and *categorically and unmistakably* we are heirs. We have hit the jackpot and the lot has been cast in our favor. Indeed, *emphatically*, *categorically*, and *unmistakably*, we have become heirs of God.

Romans 8:17 also tells us that we become joint heirs with Christ. "Joint heirs" is a compound of the Greek preposition *sun* and the Greek word *kleronomos*, which we've already learned about. To recap, the preposition *sun* means to do something *jointly* or *together with*, and it carries the idea of a partnership. The word *kleronomos* means an inheritance. It portrays *an heir* or *a lot cast in one's favor*; thus, to hit the jackpot in terms of an inheritance. In Romans 8:17, "joint heirs" literally means that we are equal or co-heirs with Jesus Christ in everything He has inherited from the Father.

The Holy Spirit Encourages Us to Take Hold of Our God-Given Inheritance

Jesus wants us to know what He possesses and what He wants to give us so much that in John 16:14, when describing the work of the Holy Spirit, Jesus said, "He shall glorify me: for he shall receive of mine, and shall shew it unto you." The word "shew" is the Greek word *anangello*, which means He will *announce* it to you, or He will *disclose* it, *divulge* it, and *proclaim* it to you. "Unto you" in Greek is the word *humin*, meaning *directly to you*. This is describing the ministry of the Holy Spirit to show you what belongs to you as a joint heir with Christ.

John 16:15 continues, "All things that the Father hath are mine: therefore said I, that he [the Holy Spirit] shall take of mine, and shall shew it unto you." Again, we see the word "shew." A better translation would be that the Holy Spirit will *announce it to you*, He will *divulge it to you*, or He will *proclaim it to you*. Everything that belongs to Jesus belongs to us, which brings us to Philippians 4:19 — a verse about *divine provision*.

Philippians 4:19 says, "But my God shall supply all your need according to his riches in glory by Christ Jesus." Again, the word "but" is the Greek word *de*, a conjunction intended to make a dramatic statement. The word "supply" is a form of the Greek word *pleroo*, which means *to completely fill* — or *to fill to the point of overflowing satisfaction, providing for all your needs*. The word "all" is an all-encompassing term meaning *leaving nothing out*. In Greek, the word "all" is plural and is the term *chreian*, which depicts *a deficit, a need, a necessity*, or even *a want*.

The Bible says "…my God shall supply all your need *according to* his riches in glory by Christ Jesus." The word "according to" in Greek is the preposition *kata*, which means *according to*, but it also carries the sense of *something that is dominating or subjugating*. Hence, this verse is saying we are to be dominated and subjugated by the riches of His glory. The word "riches," the Greek word *ploutos*, depicts *immense wealth* or *riches beyond imagination*. It pictures *one who possesses wealth so immense that it is immeasurable* or *one who has abundant riches or measureless resources*. That is what the Lord has for us, and that is what Paul was referring to when he wrote about God's riches in glory by Christ Jesus.

The following is the *Renner Interpretive Version* (*RIV*) of Philippians 4:19:

> **But my God will supply your needs so completely that He will eliminate all your deficiencies. He will meet all your physical and tangible needs until you're so full you have no more capacity to hold anything else. He will fully supply your needs until you're totally filled, packed full, and overflowing to the point of bursting at the seams and spilling over.**

That is divine provision. According to Philippians 4:19, God wants you to be dominated and subjugated by the kind of provision that is overflowing and spilling over into your life. He has made His resources available to you, but you have to access them by faith, which is what we read in Psalm 34:8. When you release your faith, you release the goodness of God — and *all of His divine provisions* — to work in your life!

STUDY QUESTIONS

> **Study to shew thyself approved unto God, a workman that needeth not to be ashamed, rightly dividing the word of truth.**
> **— 2 Timothy 2:15**

1. What do the scriptures Psalm 34:8 and Second Peter 1:3 and 4 have to do with the promises of God? How can these verses help us activate our faith and receive these promises?
2. According to Romans 8:16 and 17, what role does the Holy Spirit have in our life once we are born again? What does the Holy Spirit tell us about the precious promises of God?
3. John 16:14 says the Holy Spirit "shall receive of mine, and shall shew it unto you." What things is the Holy Spirit tasked to "shew" us? (Consider John 16:15 as you answer.)
4. Philippians 4:19 describes how abundantly God wants to provide for you. What does the Greek word *ploutos* tell us about the riches of God?

PRACTICAL APPLICATION

> **But be ye doers of the word, and not bearers only, deceiving your own selves.**
> **—James 1:22**

1. Romans 8:16 and 17 tells us that we have hit the jackpot of inheritances because we are *children of God*. Have you ever experienced a time where the Holy Spirit has witnessed to your spirit to remind you or convince you that you in fact are a child of God? Describe that experience.
2. In this lesson, we learned that we are heirs of God and joint heirs with Christ Jesus of everything that He has inherited from the Father. What does this mean for you personally?

3. Divine provision is one of the *many* promises of God given to you the moment you were saved. How have you accessed and partaken of this promise? What are some areas of your life where you need the divine provision of the Lord? Take a moment to write them down and pray for God to intervene.

Notes

Notes

Notes

CLAIM YOUR FREE RESOURCE!

As a way of introducing you further to the teaching ministry of Rick Renner, we would like to send you free of charge his teaching CD, "How To Receive a Miraculous Touch From God."

In His earthly ministry, Jesus commonly healed *all* who were sick of *all* their diseases. In this profound message, learn about the manifold dimensions of Christ's wisdom, goodness, power, and love toward all humanity who came to Him in faith with their needs.

☑ **YES, I want to receive Rick Renner's monthly teaching letter!**

Simply scan the QR code to claim this resource or go to:
renner.org/claim-your-free-offer

WITH US!

R renner.org

- facebook.com/rickrenner • facebook.com/rennerdenise
- youtube.com/rennerministries • youtube.com/deniserenner
- instagram.com/rickrrenner • instagram.com/rennerministries_
  instagram.com/rennerdenise

www.ingramcontent.com/pod-product-compliance
Lightning Source LLC
Chambersburg PA
CBHW061250040426
42444CB00010B/2337